These Around Us

These Around Us

Jon D. Lee

Kelsay Books

ISBN-13: 978-0692233566

Cover Art: Lynnette Lee

Kelsay Books
Aldrich Press
www.kelsaybooks.com

for Lynnette and Joshua

... and also for Jeannie.

With deepest respect,

JP.

27 MAR. '15

Acknowledgements

Due gratitude goes to the editors and staff of the following publications, in which some of these poems appeared, though not always in their current forms:

Clover, A Literary Rag Vol. 3: "Charon, Over an Egg and Cress Sandwich, Speaks of Ferrying the Dead," "Why You Shouldn't Become a Poet," "The Grinch"

_____ Vol. 4: "On the Departure of a Friend," "After an Evening Performance of *The Nutcracker* at Boston's Opera House," "Holding my Mother's Hand"

_____ Vol. 5: "To Whomever Left Behind The Anonymous Letter Explaining In Great Detail Exactly How Much You Loathed My Last Poetry Reading"

_____ Vol. 7: "Metempsychosis," "Why This Poem Didn't Turn Out So Good," "Newtown"

Follow The Thread: "Hand Me Down"

Hobble Creek Review Vol. 3.3: "1500-Year-Old Jardine Juniper—Logan, Utah," "Every Man A Lion"

Oregon Literary Review Vol. 4.2: "While My Wife Has Open-Heart Surgery," "Jasmine," "Eggplant Pirogue," "Still Life With Dog"

Contents

III

IV

What has been will be again,
what has been done will be done again;
there is nothing new under the sun.

—Ecclesiastes 1:9

1500-Year-Old Jardine Juniper
—Logan, Utah

Only a single, twisted curl of finger remains:
a solitary shock of green basking in evening light,
the delicate weight of needles
slowly crushing the thousand-pound arm of wood below.
So fragile an existence
this mad rush through time,
so quick the passage from then to now,
a life of darkness and light
blurring into a single memory of grey.

What promises can we make between life and death?
What oaths are there that merit our speaking them aloud,
releasing them into the wind to be borne aloft
and fall back a million,
a billion heartbeats later?

Only these,
scratched with curled fingers on our roof of sky:
here I was,
here I am,
here I will be.

I

It is spring again. The earth
is like a child that knows many poems.

—Rainer Maria Rilke, *The Sonnets to
Orpheus XXI*

Sonnet on the Moon, Rising

Calendar says full moon,
but this upturned and pale bowl
that rises against my window
seems in no hurry to fill the room
and peel back our eyes. Quarter,
half, three-quarters, light like lapping water
moves under my hand,
makes shadows in my wife's skin.
I mean it's midnight,
and I've been watching you grow
for what feels like months.
So come on out, child,
       now
I'm ready.

Reflections on a Picture of My Father

A black and white photograph hangs in my parents' home.
In it, my father, who cannot be more than twenty,
stands at the free throw line.
He bends at the knees,
elbows slightly forward,
forearms flexed at ninety degrees,
basketball cradled in both hands.
He looks so ready to move
that in my mind
the picture becomes a single cell in a movie reel
and the boy regains life, extends his arms, jumps,
snaps his right wrist forward,
follows the ball with his eyes.

We age because we are alive:
we breathe,
but the air turns bitter in our blood,
loses its electrons,
steals them from our cells to compensate,
mutates our DNA in the process;
we eat, but the sugars and proteins interact,
attach themselves to our collagen,
prevent our muscles from stretching,
leave their traces in our inflexible skin;
we move, but the motions
wear away the cartilage between our knees,
the ligaments in our feet,
the teeth in our mouth.

In the photo, my father will always remain twenty.
He won't wear away the joints in his hips,
slip the disks in his spine,
or have the knuckles in his right foot replaced with plastic.
But the boy in the photo
will also never know my mother,
never know his daughter and son,
never know how a ball can leave the fingertips,
trace a perfect path in the air,
and glide through the white net.

While My Wife Has Open-Heart Surgery

I no longer fly-fish

when last I went
casting my lure into a glass pond
in a wide Idaho meadow
I hooked a trout
too small to take away
but large enough to swallow my hook whole
hook that I yanked from her throat
driving the barbs through flesh and gill and bone
so deep was the metal
so embedded
that it could not be drawn
and all that was left me
was the snick of knife through line
and the new red line
following the silver tail
to the muck below

For Lynnette, With Love (I)

no way but this

the comma curling
of sternum and spine
in the blood pulse
before we sleep

The Expectant Father

Last night's settled dream:
five summer fingers grasping
in the morning sun.

Holding My Mother's Hand

We walk home late from a Christmas party,
the ghosts of fruitcake and wine
forming small wreaths in our breath.
I have not seen my mother since Spring,
and because of this,
and because the lights twinkle around us like Technicolor gods,
and because the course of our steps
reveals that we have had
perhaps
too much wine,
I take my mother's hand,
wrapping her smaller fingers in mine to steady our pace.
"This is nice," she says.
"You haven't held my hand since you were a kid."
Which makes me smile, and,
thinking of the lines we draw
between ourselves and others,
I grip her hand the more tightly,
holding on to what I can
as we move into the night.

Parents' Credo

For on the day you are born,
you will piss on my best dress shirt;
For by the time you are eight weeks old
I will no longer have a gag reflex,
or think twice about eating a sandwich
while changing your diaper;
For your first word will name whichever parent I am not;
For you will swallow pennies
and Lego pieces
and dead flies;
For you will sneeze,
cover your hands in grey-green globs
of virus-laden expectorant,
then feed me Cheerios;
For you will crayon a mural of unicorns and racecars
on the newly-painted living room wall;
For you will stick toothpicks in electric outlets;
For you will shove Skittles up your nose;
For, while I am phoning my parents
to tell of the day you learned to ride a bike,
the smoke detector will inform me
that you have also learned
the orange-bright wonder of matches;
For you will give your younger sister a haircut;
For, a week later, you will give the dog a haircut;
For I will lose count of the nights I wake from sweaty dreams
of you drowning in the bathtub,
suffocating on grocery bags,

having your fingers gnawed off by the dog,
discovering the soft pink objects in our nightstand drawers,
discovering the red purpose of a knife;
For I will pay for your first speeding ticket,
and the insurance,
and the car,
and the oil changes,
and the gas;
For I will pay for your first date,
then lie awake until you come home at midnight;
For, in the end, you will leave,
and the house will echo its silence and deafen me.

For all of these reasons will I feed you.
For all of these reasons will I clothe you.
For all of these reasons,
when the thunderclaplightningstrike
sends you shrieking to my bed
will I hold you,
tangle my fingers in your hair,
and whisper your name until again you sleep.

Still Life With Dog

Suspended in mid-air
and mid-yap
a Sheltie bounds over rocks
in pursuit of a three-point Texas Whitetail buck
on the other side of a metal fence
only the latter can clear

oblivious to the prisons of small jaw and small leg
fixed on the white and black flashes
of tail and hoof
the dog's mouth lolls open
as if to say
I'll get you, you sonofabitch

someday

For the Mouse I Carried Out of the Bathroom Last Night

Does it matter, my carrying the trembling body into
rays of moonlight, hearing the feet
meet pebble and grass, what I thought a laugh at new-
found freedom? Did it find shelter in
sod and twig? Seek
longer grasses, deep earth, enough seeds to
tease its palate? Or did it find the owl, slide
down its throat, discover a different darkness?

After an Evening Performance of *The Nutcracker* at Boston's Opera House

It was wicked good
especially when they brought out all the little kids
in their fancy dresses
and had 'em run around the stage bangin' on drums
and I liked how the clock in the back
was actually a real clock
and not one of those painted-on things that look fake
and the part in the middle
where they had that big Christmas tree that just grew
and grew until it hit the ceiling was pretty neat
must of done it by wires or gears under the floor
at least that part you couldn't tell how it was done
unlike when that sleigh came out of the roof
and carried 'em all off
that part you could just see the wires
that coulda been done better
but for the most part it was wicked good
what I don't understand is how this is a show for kids
I mean there were tons of 'em onstage
and the audience was filled with 'em
and most of the time they were even pretty quiet
but some of them dancers weren't wearing a whole lot
or exactly leaving much to the imagination
if you know what I mean
like that guy who played the Nutcracker
and came out wearing that big mask

that guy was only wearing a little pair of white tights
and stuff bounces around you know
and when he was doing all those leaps and twirls
it was pretty hard not to look
I mean I know it was supposed to be pretty and all
and I'm not gay
but every time that guy moved
all I could think about was junk and ass
and it kinda ruined the show

On Overly-Tanned Young Women

How lovely you are when the day is done:
A raisin, resplendent, and dyed by the sun.

Elegy for a Scuba Diver
—Edmund's Ferry, WA

By the time he lay on dry sand
it was far too late:
forty feet down,
secure in wet suit, oxygen tank,
respirator, and life vest,
his heart stopped.

I often wonder his final moments:
blood stilling
in veins surrounded by currents of salt water;
the slow horizontal ship-like roll of body;
a final breath rising to the surface,
expanding,
exploding.

II

And so with the sunshine and the great bursts of leaves growing on the trees, just as things grow in fast movies, I had that familiar conviction that life was beginning over again with the summer.

—F. Scott Fitzgerald, *The Great Gatsby*

Metempsychosis

The plurality that we perceive is only an appearance; it is not real
—Erwin Schrödinger, "The Mystic Vision"

Here says the doctor
handing to arms not my own
yet which spring from my shoulders
a swaddled bundle
from which stare eyes so familiar
I cannot place them
in my voice someone says *It's a boy*
and the woman on the table
whose insides spill from the incision
like the words hanging around us
begins to laugh
and cry
while in my hands
this mirror
that is not a mirror
stares back at me
opens a mouth I cannot tell is not mine
and fills the world with song

Bowl Turning—Pasadena, Newfoundland

Sawdust cloaks our breath
rinds our eyes
encrusts our fingers
smothers our hair
muffles the floor
flakes the mouths of the beer bottles that line the workbench

on the lathe a block of white birch
becomes a cylinder
becomes an inverted cone
becomes a bowl

the chisel jumps in my unlined hands
snarls against the grain
pits and cracks the wood
but my father-in-law's pitted and cracked hands
smooth my mistakes
hover against the drone of engine belts
like a watchful pilot
on the edge of this island
on the edge of the earth
as all around us
the world turns in larger
and far less perfect circles

For Lynnette, With Love (II)

the hiss of skin
as you slide through white sheets
pulls me from slumber
reminds me that some things
are better than dreams

The Lovers' Song

Mark how one string, sweet husband to another,
Strikes each in each by mutual ordering;
Resembling sire and child and happy mother,
Who, all in one, one pleasing note do sing
　　　　　—William Shakespeare, Sonnet 8

Sing now a song:
a song of day and night,
of oak and linden,
of root and earth.
Sing now a song:
a song of sun and moon,
of earth and sky,
of heart and hand.
Sing now a song:
a song of stones worn smooth by lapping waters,
of rivers that carve their gentle trenches through mountains,
of stars that burn and fill the sky with light.
Sing now a song:
a song of things that once were divided but are now whole,
of fingers that twine with fingers in the dark,
of voices that rise and meet as one.
Sing now a song:
a song of things the way they were,
of things the way they are,
and of the paths that led them to where they belong.
Sing now a song:
a song that begins on the tongue, but rises from the heart,
a song that has neither beginning nor end,
a song that knows not sorrow, but joy.

Sing now a song:
a song bound neither by language nor time,
a song unfrozen by winter's descent,
a song that pulses like fire in the blood.
Sing now a song:
in a chorus of voices that fills up our lives
with a beat and a music that pulses and drives,
for the love that we nurture is the love that survives—
so sing now this song, for when properly tended,
love creates notes by which all things are mended,
and songs that keep playing when the music has ended.

—For Ryan and Abbie

On Writing This Poem

Well, that's shit!
—Bill Holm

By the time I realized its presence
the ingrown hair was days old
an irritation under my jaw
sliding between layers of skin

no effort could bring it forth
no tweezer was fine enough to wrench the shaft
no pin sharp enough to dig and lever
sheet after sheet of toilet paper sopped with blood
until finally a small curl broke free
then snapped in half
and sunk back into its pore
where it snarled for a week
festering and raw
distending the parchment of my neck
reminding me of its pregnancy
with every turn of my head
every glance in the mirror

until at last it revealed itself
and grasping it
I drew it forth
held its glistening form up to the ruddy bathroom light
for one triumphant moment
then flushed it down the drain

The Grinch

The Gingriches divorced last year after Marianne found out about Newtie's cutie—Callista Bisek, a congressional aide with whom Newt had a long-running affair.

Gingrich asked for the divorce by phoning his wife on Mother's Day, 1999.

Jackie Battley, Newt's first wife, was hospitalized for cancer treatment in 1981 when Newt told her he wanted a divorce.
                    —as printed in the *New York Post,* July 18, 2000

What you must remember about changing diapers
is three things

First
if you're changing a boy
be sure to put a cloth over his penis when the diaper is off
because the cold air on his belly is going to make him pee
and if that cloth isn't there
you're going to get a mouthful

Second
you're dealing with an immature gastrointestinal tract
that doesn't know how to control itself
and all of the waste will be liquid
until the baby gets on solid foods
so when you're holding your baby's legs up to wipe its bottom
watch out
I've seen kids crap so hard
the blowout hit the opposite side of the room

Third
when you put the clean diaper on
make sure it's on right
pulled up all the way
the elastics tight against the skin
because if there are any loose spots or gaps
that's where the poop is going to come out
and if your kid has one of those blowouts
and that diaper isn't on right
then you could be standing in line at the grocery store
or in a fancy restaurant
and you're suddenly gonna be covered in shit
and when that happens
because it will
to every one of you
at least once
you better hope you packed a change of clothes

As for the ones you're wearing
well
you can try to soak them in detergent and hot water
before you put them in the washing machine
and you're going to want to use
a second rinse cycle when you do
but keep in mind that some things can't be saved
and even if it's a two hundred dollar blouse
or a five hundred dollar suit
sometimes it's best just to throw it in the trash
and move on

For Lynnette, With Love (III)

in my haste
a single saline sphere slipped
through fingers and tissue
as I clumsily smeared your cheek
skimmed lip and jawline
plunged through an abyss of time
collided with the hardwood floor
in a cacophony
of noise and freckled light
mea culpa
mea culpa

The Poet's Retort

I do hereby renounce the last poem I
Wrote about you. These words instead will be
Printed in my book. My love has died:
A rotted soldier's corpse at Normandy.
No more "Shall I compare thee to...," no more
"But soft! What light...." No more young lovers, arms
Entwined, a gross groping of diseased whores
Or syphilitic teenagers. Your charms
Are gone, your beauty faded. Here you stand:
Exposed, soiled harpy, nature's inexact
And pregnant beast, a wrinkled hag, one hand
On withered tit. Do I overreact?
My love has died. Yourself to blame, my dear:
How dare you take the last can of cold beer?

Conversation Overheard in a University Bathroom

This,
secreting beneath brown-and-graffiti stall doors,
held in counterpoint
by the staccato toccata of flagrant splashing,
yellow tile walls resounding with savoir-faire,
the air heavy in exuberant ablutions:
"I don't know why I'm failing my classes,
mom.
None of my teachers like me."

Gorilla Cage

Only breath divides us
father from father
one whose arms secure a child yet too weak to walk
the other watches a son scamper and squeal at his knees
For a moment we meet
then slide away into our own lives
and I wonder
if challenged
whose hand would be the faster to rise
crack a stick on the other's skull
pry open the thin rind
between what we know and who we are

Letter of Resignation

Cogito, ergo sum
>—René Descartes, *Principles of Philosophy* (1644)

Lasciate ogne speranza, voi ch'intrate
>—Dante Alighieri, *Inferno* Canto 3 (14th century)

Not poppy, nor mandragora,
Nor all the drowsy syrups of the world,
Shall ever med'cine thee to that sweet sleep
Which thou owedst yesterday.
>—William Shakespeare, *Othello* 3.3.330-333 (c. 1603)

professor John,

Hi I noticed that my final grade in ur English class is a D- I was wondering what I did to earn that grade I know I was absent a lot from ur class and missed several quizs and didn't turn in my final paper but I didn't think it would effect my grade like that could u please tell me what I did wrong I would appreciate it also if there is any extra credit I could do to make it up please let me know I'm planning on transferring to another college next semester could u please write me a letter of recommendation and talk about my god work ethic I would appreciate that to u can just send the letter to me and I'll send it off to the school's I'm applying too also ps I rely enjoyed ur class u were very funny and smart its just to bad ur class was at 8 am that's a really hard time to get up and that's why I missed a lot of ur classes ok let me know what u think and I will hear back from u soon I hope u enjoy ur xmas break and ur family is well :)

Sent from my iPhone

Crosses and Noughts

It was never a question
of what to do with you in life.
But there, in the office,
with its white walls
and washable steel tables,
standing over what remained,
it became my choice to decide the rest.

You were lighter,
after the fire. So thin
that the box you came in
almost rose through my fingers
and the ceiling,
pulling at the air,
as if what departed in smoke
was still whole.

In the car,
you sat on the front seat—
like always—
window down and the a/c on high.
And somehow we made it back,
walked through the door together,
returned to the only place
we ever called home

III

Another fall, another turned page: there
was something of jubilee in that annual
autumnal beginning, as if last year's
mistakes had been wiped clean by summer.

—Wallace Stegner, *Angle of Repose*

To My Wife, On Her First Mother's Day

I woke last night to the steadiness of your breath
A lull and rush like the whispers of a heart
In the next room our child stirred
Cried out softly in sleep and murmured nonsense
For a lifetime I lay there
Following the music as it filled the room with light
And drove away the shadows of the dawn

Crosswalk

The evidence trails halfway behind me before I see them:
the mother, kneeling to point
at the raised red hand that glows over my shoulder,
her sentence a cold hammering of reason—
"It means don't walk, honey,
it's too dangerous and you might get hurt"—
and the daughter,
who stares at neither mother nor hand,
but instead locks eyes with me.
In the moment before I look away,
I notice that she cannot be much older than my son,
and that I am just as much her father as anyone.
Then the walls fall again between us,
and these bars,
whose crisp edges once clipped neatly beneath me,
black and white and black and white,
blur into a gray and rising haze
that obscures the faultless horizon.

Jasmine

3-year-olds neither plan for the future
nor live completely in the present.
Instead, they call up the past as they need it.
—Proceedings of the National Academy of Sciences

At Christmas I clipped the hasp
of a dog leash to my belt loop
and gave the handle to my not-quite-two-year-old niece
who stared for a moment at the blue nylon fibers
then squealing scuttled through living room and kitchen
dining room and pantry
over chairs
under tables
three times around the dog
between her grandmother's legs
into the tub
out of the tub
yelling "Running! Running! Running!"
the walls rebounding with her shrieks
and I as the world's heaviest balloon
rebounding from those walls
stocking feet sliding on Saltillo tile
watching as we round a new corner
the rope jumping
slipping behind the porcelain doll on the low table
my hand stretching to catch the figure halfway to the floor
careful to not yet let the present
come crashing down around us

Stop-loss

Each day
the yellow carnations
in the blue vase in our kitchen
wither imperceptibly,
bend slowly under the weight of time.
Their petalskins mottle and discolor,
fold helplessly into indelible crenellations.
Strange knots plague their stemjoints.
The tissues desiccate,
once-strong tendrils
now clabber against the rim for support.
And yet,
and yet,
when I leaned over them this morning
to gather the bits of their bodies
that fell during the night, a hint,
the merest shade of perfume
consumed me.

The Botanist's Prayer

Lord,
please reserve a special place in hell
for he who thought up the name
Horny Goat Weed
and consigned us all
to the eternal tittering of freshmen.
May his stamen wither
and his pollen fall on barren pistil.
May tubers grow from his testicles,
inchworms infest his armpits,
and Powderpost beetles ravage his pith
until he collapses under his own heady weight.
Amen.

Why This Poem Didn't Turn Out So Good

We apologize for the inconvenience.
—Douglas Adams, *So Long, and Thanks for All the Fish*

I have apparently perturbed my waiter.
Unused, perhaps,
to someone who wishes simply to sit alone,
with a pint,
in a far corner,
and stare not at book, notepad, phone, or computer,
but long and hard and without madness
at the distances between *what* and *why*,
he has taken to pausing at every passing,
asking if I want more beer
(though my glass is but half empty)
or a menu
(though I have expressed no desire for food)
or how I thought the game was last night,
or the traffic this morning,
or the weather this afternoon.
"I'm writing a poem," I want to tell him,
"Go away."
But I suspect this will not have its intended effect.
"About what?" he'll reply, or,
"Stuck on a rhyme?" or,
though we both already know the answer,
"Written anything I might have read?"
So instead I nod, smile, say "yes" and "no,"
my answers simple and without elaboration,
extracting me delicately from this man,
this conversation,
this bar,

impelling me back into the maelstrom of my thoughts,
where I am drawn ever inwards—
closer, closer, closer—
to the only voice whose answers I can trust.

An Epistle Written to John Stuart Mill after 24.9 Inches of Snow Fell in Boston, MA in Less Than 24 Hours on February 8-9, 2013

Hey mister, you need help shoveling that snow?
What?
You need help? You gotta long driveway and you just started.
Sure, if you want to.
Twenty bucks.
What?
Twenty bucks. You start on that end, we'll start over here,
    we'll have this cleared in twenty minutes. We got two
        shovels, we work fast.
No, thanks anyways.
Your loss, mister.

Hey mister!
Hey guys.
You sure you don't want help, mister?
I'm halfway done by now, guys.
Yeah, but it's more snow on this end where the plow came
    through.
That's okay, I'll get to it.
You sure work fast, mister.
I lived in Newfoundland for a while. I've had a lot of practice.
Where?
Newfoundland. It's a province in Canada.

A what?

It's kind of like a state.

Oh. Fifteen bucks, mister. We'll have this clean in fifteen
minutes.

No, but thank you. Listen, if you want to help someone out,
go next door.

Where?

That one. The lady who lives there is ninety years old and
in the hospital. I'm sure she'd like a clean driveway
when she gets back.

Thanks, mister!

Hey mister!

Yeah, guys.

There's nobody home.

What?

At the old lady's house. Nobody answered the door.

No, I told you boys, she's in the hospital.

When's she gettin' out?

Well, she's in there for anemia, but we're hoping pretty soon.

But she's not coming home today?

No, I don't think so.

Oh. You sure you don't need help?

No, thank you. I'm almost done anyway.

Yeah, but there's a little left. Ten bucks, mister, we'll be done in
five minutes. We got two shovels. We work fast.

For Lynnette, With Love (IV)

even the sea is jealous
rushing forward in frothy foam
to taste the site
where your lips meet mine

Charon, Over an Egg and Cress Sandwich, Speaks of Ferrying the Dead

Maggots and mongrels every one,
sobbing as they stain the boards of my boat,
mewling in their mucous,
begging as they besmear my once-clear waters
with their slurry of piss and vomit.
Eventually, they all must pass me:
philosophers and idiots,
sane men and the mad,
rulers and the ruled.
But as it is their curse to meet me,
so too is it mine to meet them:
sailors reproving my rickety raft;
tailors criticizing the cut of my cloth;
old men complaining of their prostates;
old women complaining of their old men.
What could they possibly know of such things,
these people whose ribcages
have never resounded with the bite of rusty blades,
whose distended abdomens
come not from disease and dysentery,
but gluttony and drunkenness?
What could anyone know of loss
who has not shepherded the day-old child
discarded in the waste bin,
knowing that no one awaits it at the barren docks,
knowing that its bed will forever be pebbles and debris,
knowing
that when the crack and groan

of wood and paddle
have finally lulled it into bliss,
that it will turn in its blindness and hunger
to suckle at your thin breast,
and you will have nothing to offer
but ashes and dust.

On Feeling Sorry for One's Self

Consider a woodpecker,
starving, in search of food,
slamming the hollow shard of its shattered beak
against the bark of a fallen oak,
the impotent dents left behind
the punch line of an empty joke:
knock knock,
knock knock.

Newtown

—in memoriam, 12/14/12

Between my knees,
my seventeen-month-old son sits astride a rubber horse,
one hand wrapped around a raised cartoon ear,
the other wrapped in mine.
He bounces and shrieks,
fills the room with noise and light,
his calls a welcome salvo,
his motions a suture in time.
Suddenly the horse bucks—
as horses will do—
and spills him onto the floor,
and though my hand breaks his fall,
this laughing world collapses,
these toys and dreams turn dark and hollow.
So I pick my son from the rubble
and place him on my knee,
where I wipe the salt water from his cheeks
and whisper comforts in his ear.
And if today I hold him more tightly,
brush his hair more gently,
then this world is a better place for it.

The Old Man and the Truth

Here lies an old man you never knew,
and now you never will, you jerk.
        "The Old Man Orders His Tombstone"
        —Ken Brewer, November 28, 1941—March 15, 2006

How like one of your own poems, your story:
how, when showering at your son's,
your foot slipped on the white acrylic
and you crumpled to the floor,
clawed at the curtains,
drug shampoo and soap from their ceremonial ledges,
dislodged the curtain rod,
stubbed your toe on the fixtures,
cracked your ribs on the rim, your scalp on the sink,
ended up balled on the floor,
bawling for help, your modesty preserved
only by the coincidental leaning
of the bottle of body wash. Or how,
when the daughter-in-law who had just divorced your son
confronted you with her newly-lifted breasts
and asked you to evaluate them,
you stared at the stretch marks
and stitched nipples and purple bruises
and said only, "...They're nice." Or how, at the end,
when cancer had taken first one decade of your life,
then another,
you sat with me in your porch swing,
portacath in your thin chest

visible through your unbuttoned shirt,
and held my hand as we talked
and watched the sun set over the Wasatch Mountains,
your touch somehow more intimate than a lover's.
In the red glare of that last evening
I glimpsed in the glass patio door
your reflection, bearded and smiling,
pale and drawn,
lovely in the last year of your life.

IV

I wonder if the snow loves the trees
and fields, that it kisses them so gently?
And then it covers them up snug,
you know, with a white quilt; and perhaps
it says *Go to sleep, darlings, till the summer
comes again.*

— Lewis Carroll, *Alice's Adventures
in Wonderland & Through the Looking-Glass*

Sick

In my arms my son mewls in fevered sleep,
arches a mountain range of spine
and soaks his sweat through my shirt.
On the counter the thermometer reads 103,
and though my son is not yet two,
his blood already knows the taste of fire,
courses halfway to boiling in his veins.
He jerks, shudders,
his dreams a red and oil-less engine
that screams in the dark,
and I, who can do little but hush and hum,
nevertheless press his frame into mine
as if drawing poison from a wound,
or fervor from the smoldering cinder
of a body too brittle to burn so bright,
a world too small to swallow such flame.

Eggplant Pirogue

We work in tandem—
an assembly line of two—
I, peeling the eggplants
and placing those peels
in a sack we will later throw to the deer,
and my father, who whittles what's left
into suitable hollows.
Our knuckles brush occasionally
as they pass over the grocery bag.
The wine in the bottle to our left moves toward the floor,
keeping pace and color with the sun.
We work in silence, hand over hand,
creased brow and smooth,
wreathed in purple trailings
in the fading December light.

To the Little Girl at the Poetry Reading

When I rise from myself
to stare at this room
its pure white ceiling slipping
into pure white walls covered
with paintings of grasses you cannot touch
and grazing cattle you cannot hear

when I tilt my head
to better catch the machine-gun prattle
of the grey-headed man behind the podium
whose words are stained scarlet
as he decries a war that ended long before you were born

when I shift my hips
against the iron maiden that is this metal seat
crossing and uncrossing
and crossing my legs
to the buzzing tempo of my sleeping feet

I do not question
when you cry aloud in the middle of a stanza
"Daddy, I don't like it here!"
and kick your chair

Come
take my hand
let us wander far from here
to wonder at real cows feeding in real fields
the roughness of tree bark against bare feet
and the way
if you hold your hand just so
even the largest mountains fit in your palm

For Lynnette, With Love (V)

I could study forever
the intricate constellations
that freckle your skin
knowing
that if I ever lost myself in their answers
you would lead me home

The Lovers' Dance

When you do dance, I wish you
A wave o' th' sea, that you might ever do
Nothing but that.
—William Shakespeare, *The Winter's Tale* 4.4.159-161

When you meet, it will be spring,
and the first tentative touches
will be as warm breath on glass.
The music will be slow, hesitant,
but do not let this stop you.
Take your partner.
Marvel at the drape of her hand on your shoulder,
the firmness of his arms around your waist,
the meeting of thigh and hip.
As you begin to sway,
you will find you do not know the steps.
This is not important.
It is enough, for now, to simply feel, and be, and move.

Then it will be summer,
and while the steps by now will be more familiar,
they will also be wilder and more intricate:
the lull and sway of the slow dance
replaced by the playfulness of the pirouette,
and the energy of the swing.
There will still be much to learn,
but much to gain from the learning:
each turn of wrist an indelible moment,
each sweep of foot an irreplaceable memory;
each twining of fingers and arms,
each meeting of eye and eye
a merging of form and function, of self and self,

until what was once not you becomes you,
becomes the mirror in which you think and see and feel,
becomes the body and face
that is more yours than your own.
Let the dance take you, carry you over stone and river,
above valley and mountain, across ocean and continent,

carry you through summer and into fall,
where the leaves will fall
in a ballet of orange and umber and gold,
carry you as the world spins dizzily around your own ballet,
carry you deep into the forest and far across the field
where a pale bulge of moon rises against a distant horizon,

carry you into the stately waltz of winter,
where stars will lash the circumference of a crisp sky
and the silver-gray snow
will cloak your shoulders like a blush of hair.
And only when the last star winks out in the sky,
when the moon slips below the horizon
and the world is dark,
then, and only then, will you be allowed to stop.

But not to let go.
For there are steps that outlast the shuffling of tired feet,
gestures that extend beyond the compass
of an outstretched hand,
and notes that continue to play
long after the music has ended.

—For Navin and Lori

Directions Short and Simple

The hiss and slip of soft-soled shoes
announces the presence of the old man and his wife
long before they shuffle into view.
They round the corner near the prescription desk,
scan store shelves for liniments and bandages,
creams and razors,
cluck their tongues at prices,
mumble over the measurements of milliliters and grams.
I cannot tell which of them has the greater need,
each somehow clutching the arm of the other for support,
dual delicate flying buttresses of porous bone.
It is not difficult to imagine the consequence of loss:
two bent towers sinking into earth
when only one has faltered.

What great peace
this manner of life must bring,
as in the scuttle of seawater on sand,
as in the golden seep of hummingbird beak into nectar,
as in the calmness of your hand as it slips into mine.

To Whomever Left Behind The Anonymous Letter Explaining In Great Detail Exactly How Much You Loathed My Last Poetry Reading

Sir/Madam,

While I recognize that what follows will be
an imperfect vehicle in responding to your concerns—
since it is safe to assume that,
following my reading,
you did not purchase one of my books,
and are unlikely to purchase one in the future
(avoiding, for the moment,
the larger discussion of whether you have ever
bought a book of poetry),
and are thus unlikely to ever read this—
I have little choice but to respond in such fashion,
the anonymity of your letter
having precluded other courses of action,
and while "I do not like the office" (*Othello* 3:3:410),
I find it necessary to respond in brief
to certain of your claims.

I find it, however, difficult to locate my beginnings,
as the confused grammar of your opening address,
which inexplicably lacks both a predicate and,
somehow, verbs,
(an accomplishment unparalleled in academic discourse),
makes it unclear whether you are referring to me,
or to my reading, or to my poetry, or to all three,
as a "shitbag." Regardless,

please be informed that this constitutes
an *Ad Hominem* logical fallacy,
which is Latin for "to the man,"
but used in this context indicates a response that attacks
not the logic of the original assertions,
but the character of the arguer,
and should thus obviously be avoided.
As for the comprehensible sections of your statements,
the denotation of "Christomimetic"
(note the correct spelling)
is "in imitation of Christ" or "Christ-like,"
and not, as you seem to have inferred,
"making fun of Jesus,"
and your conceptions of hell
are mistakenly based
upon what is widely recognized as, in part,
a mistranslation of the Greek word "Gehenna,"
which was a valley outside ancient Jerusalem where,
according to folklore (but unsubstantiated by archaeology),
fires were kept eternally burning
to dispose of rubbish and animal corpses
and, occasionally, criminals,
and while brimstone
(note the correct spelling)
was added to keep the fires burning,
the usage of this location in the bible
is more figurative than literal,
and our modern conceptions of hell
seem to stem largely from the Middle Ages,

influenced perhaps most heavily
by the Italian poet Dante Alighieri (1265-1321)
in his *magnum opus*, *Inferno*
(cf. Lee; Lee and Monarch; Lee and Turner).

Finally, while you must recognize
the anatomically improbable nature
of your closing imperative-reflexive phrase,
it might interest you to know
that the verb used therein is etymologically fascinating,
in large part because its taboo nature
has resulted in few scholars attempting
to unravel its etymology
until fairly recently. The OED
(or Oxford English Dictionary)
dates the earliest appearance
of the printed form of the word to 1503,
in the form *fukkit*,
though other sources note that the word appears—
though heavily coded as "gxddbov"
because of its taboo nature—
in the 15th century poem "Flen Flyys,"
a code which, when easily broken
by substituting the preceding letter of the alphabet
(bearing in mind the differences
between premodern and modern alphabets),
gives "fuccant." The word is, however, undoubtedly older,
with some scholars claiming it derives
from the Norwegian *fukka*, meaning "copulate,"
and others noting its resemblance to Middle Dutch *fokken*,

or German *ficken*,
early uses of which translate to "itch" or "scratch,"
either of which provides an anatomically possible action
that is certainly more compatible with your suggestion!

Now that such awkwardness has passed,
I am glad that we better understand each other.
But let us not become complacent in this nirvana,
for while, in this postmodern era,
we must accede to the rupturing of the syntagmatic
and the multiplicity of smaller narratives,
we must still recognize the valuation
of knowledge and grammar,
and perhaps most saliently,
remind ourselves daily
that solipsism recapitulates arrogance.

Cordially,

Dr. Jon D. Lee, M.A., B.A., Ph.D.
(please note the correct spelling)
Adjunct Professor
English Department

For Lynnette, With Love (VI)

in the white heart of winter
when even the sugarblood
of tree and bush
ceases its languid
spill and thump
I ask only
for the fever of your breath

On the Departure of a Friend

Such a silly worry:
the absence of a scant few trillion cells,
the odd pound or three of carbon,
an ounce of magnesium,
a measure of intestine.
Who is there to notice this missing leg,
this absent hand,
this empty stomach,
this misplaced heart?
Certainly not these people who surround me,
these ideations who move from sterile pocket to sterile pocket,
tripping over sidewalk cracks as they talk to their phones.
"Fuck," they say,
"It's only fucking Monday afternoon?"
As if the world owes them respite,
still holds the change from their purchase,
has somehow miscalculated the balance
between what has been given
and what has been taken away.

—For the Great Southern Man

Hand Me Down

Just inside this room
where my grandparents slept a third of their lives
a white plastic horse gallops across a savannah of bed sheets
Lone Ranger astride straight back
hand on pistol
hat on head

Just inside this room
where my grandmother combed her hair gray
an oversized yellow safety razor
scrapes its rubber blade over chin and arm and chest
leaves mountains of invisible stubble
to prickle a child's bare feet

Just inside this room
where my grandfather did not wake up
a red plastic mallet bashes bed lumps flat
beats back the darkness behind the door

Just inside this room
where my mother was conceived
my mother gathers my toys in a yellow bin
drives them halfway across the country
and places them carefully so that
just inside
this room
my waking son may shout his surprise
fill the house with clatter and joy
his exaltations free of import
unburdened by lesson and truth

Waiting Room

No, he's not my father.
He lives down the street and I take care of him.
He's eighty-four
and still an active judge,
though he's obviously slowed.
Rumor is he'll be forced into early retirement this summer.
It's only in the last year he's gotten this way.
The cancer did it:
pancreatic, a grape-sized bulb found last month.
He's in here now for a CAT scan
so they can figure out how much
of the pancreatic lobe they want to chop off,
and if they have to take his spleen too.
'Course, that means there's not much time left.

Nicest man you'll ever meet.
He's a World War Two vet,
fought at the Battle of the Bulge,
the bloodiest series of battles in the whole war,
and at one of those battles,
where the Germans mined a bridge to explode
to stop the Allied forces from advancing,
he was one of the soldiers who ran across that bridge,
got to the other side through the snow
and a wall of machine gun fire
and dug himself in.
He's never talked about it.
The only reason I know
is he's got a picture on his wall
of him in front of that bridge,
and all the medals in his display case.

In fact, as I understand it,
he's only ever told one story about the War,
and that story was one sentence long.
One of his sons joined ROTC,
got shipped to Germany in the '70s
and spent four years in active duty.
One day his whole troop
took a field trip to the concentration camps
so they could see what happens when the world goes bad,
and why the Army does the work it does.
So his son, over dinner,
after he got back to the States,
was telling his dad about this trip,
how they showed them the shoes
and where the mass graves were,
and the barbed wire,
and the showers,
and then they took them all back to the ovens
and opened the doors.
And his son said he had to shut his eyes when they did,
sure that when those doors opened
there'd be something in there.
But of course there wasn't.
They'd been cleaned out,
scrubbed,
made safe for tourists.

And that's when his dad spoke up,
and said the only thing he ever said about the War:
"That's not what was behind those doors when I opened them."

Hell of a way to go, cancer.

Every Man A Lion

beside you someone whose hand you'd recognize
in any degree of darkness holding your hand,
wristbone connected to the armbone,
and though you don't know how this world began
or how it might end,
you know the pathway that leads to repose
                    "Hands"
                    —William Kloefkorn, August 12, 1932—May 19, 2011

On my thirteenth birthday
you sent a lion
carved out of felled wood
gathered in your Nebraska backyard,
wood that I imagine you curled over on your porch,
surrounded by curled shavings
falling from the sharp pocketknife in your right hand,
the oils of your left hand
staining the carving a yellow August sun.

A letter was paired with the lion,
and though that letter has long since decayed
from the oils of my fingers,
I remember the words:
you, pausing in the fifty-seventh celebration of your life
to help me celebrate mine,
a pair of birthdays,
man and child hand in hand
in these golden August summers.
"Every man a fucking Leo!" you said.
"Every man a fucking lion!"

Last summer
was your last birthday,
seventy-eight-year-old body made brittle by time,
felled by disease.
I could not make your celebration,
but you made mine.
And when the news came in,
I gathered our wooden lion—
now brittle,
but golden with age—
and cradled its weight in both hands,
man and child,
lest it too fall,
and I lose all the words I have left of you.

Life's but a walking shadow, a poor player
That struts and frets his hour upon the stage
And then is heard no more. It is a tale
Told by an idiot, full of sound and fury,
Signifying nothing.

—William Shakespeare, Macbeth 5:5:23-27

Why You Shouldn't Become a Poet
—New England, Fall

for the past few weeks
the hundred-foot-tall oak in my backyard
has dropped its seeds on lawn and roof
the clonk and ping of acorn meat on tin portico
the dying systole of September

just last week the leaves turned
verdant plumes exploding
in dried cascades of raw umber, burnt ochre, vermilion

in their winter coats
grey-backed squirrels grow ever more round and chittery
littering porch rails with spent husks
filling branch nooks with thick nests
hiding acorns in tall grasses and under leaves

such wonder in this scene
such symmetry
each action purposed for survival
each motion a prayer for life
and all of it
just today
I lawnmowered into forty-eight brown paper yard bags
and placed on the curb

About the Author

Jon D. Lee has a Ph.D. in Folklore, and is the author of the collection of poems *Ode to Brian: The Long Season,* and the academic monograph *An Epidemic of Rumors: How Stories Shape our Perceptions of Disease.* He lectures at various universities in Boston, MA, where he lives with his wife and son.